SESAME STREET Autism Connections

Furry Friendships

Animals as Friends and Helpers

Leslie Kimmelman

Lerner Publications ◆ Minneapolis

Alongside friends from *Sesame Street*, children will explore how we all experience the world in unique ways—from developing friendships and flexible thinking to how we communicate and receive support. This series celebrates all children, helping young readers and their grown-ups appreciate the amazing qualities in everyone, fostering greater understanding.

Sincerely,
the Editors at Sesame Workshop

Table of Contents

Animal Pals

Furry friends can be the best of friends. They can be great helpers too.

Rose!

Helpful Friends

Some animals are specially trained to help people. Many of them are therapy animals. Some therapy animals visit people in hospitals or nursing homes.

Slimey isn't furry or specially trained, but he makes me happy—I mean, grouchy.

Animal pals may make it easier to meet new friends. They can be something to talk about!

People always want to know more about my bird friend, Bernice.

Riding horses can help you grow stronger and feel calmer and more confident.

Music can help you feel calm and confident too!

Reading to a furry friend is good practice. Furry friends can be good listeners.

Happy!

Caring for furry friends is a big responsibility. They need food and water, brushing and bathing, and exercise.

Elmo and Tango love to go for walks together.

Sometimes it's nice to just be together quietly. Your furry friend may help you feel better when you're sad or worried. You may make them feel better too!

My furry friend is my teddy bear, Radar. Do you have a friend like Radar?

Remember to be gentle with your animal pal. What do they like? Tummy tickles? Scratching behind their ears?

Hooray for fantastic furry friends!

Your Turn!

My Awesome Animal Pal

Which of these animal pals would you like as a pet or helper? Why? What would you do together?

Glossary

confident: having or showing belief in yourself

hospital: a place where sick or injured people go to get care

nursing home: a place where care is provided for people who are unable to care for themselves

therapy animal: an animal that is specially trained to help people

Read More

Cook, Jennifer. *My Friend Julia: A Sesame Street® Book about Autism*. Lerner Publications, 2024.

Koestler-Grack, Rachel A. *Therapy Horses*. Jump!, 2024.

Lilley, Matt. *Therapy Dogs*. Apex, 2023.

Index

Photo Acknowledgments

Image credits: Mayur Kakade/Getty Images, p. 4; Erik Isakson/Getty Images, p. 6 (left); Jim Craigmyle/Getty Images, p. 6 (right); Tatiana Cheremukhina/Getty Images, p. 8; Kristian Bell/Getty Images, p. 9; CasarsaGuru/Getty Images, p. 10; Africa Studio/Shutterstock, p. 12; SolStock/Getty Images, p. 14; Westend61/Getty Images, p. 16; StefaNikolic/Getty Images, p. 18; Genadi Yakovlev/500px/Getty Images, p. 20 (dog); Anja Strubel/500px/Getty Images, p. 20 (mouse); Anton Nikitinskiy/Shutterstock, p. 20 (rabbit); eugenehill/Shutterstock, p. 20 (cat); Kerrick/Getty Images, p. 20 (hamster); Doug Wilson/Getty Images, p. 20 (goldfish); Aleksandr Zubkov/Getty Images, p. 20 (teddy bear); Abrar Shadid/Shutterstock, p. 20 (horse).

Lerner Publications Company
An imprint of Lerner Publishing Group, Inc.
241 First Avenue North
Minneapolis, MN 55401 USA

For reading levels and more information, look up this title at www.lernerbooks.com.

Main body text set in Mikado a.
Typeface provided by HvD Fonts.

Editor: Annie Zheng **Designer:** Mary Ross
Lerner team: Martha Kranes

Library of Congress Cataloging-in-Publication Data

The Cataloging-in-Publication Data for *Furry Friendships: Animals as Friends and Helpers* is on file at the Library of Congress.
ISBN 979-8-7656-8511-2 (lib. bdg.)
ISBN 979-8-3480-2923-4 (pbk.)
ISBN 979-8-7656-9834-1 (epub)

Manufactured in the United States of America
1-1012744-54587-7/14/2025